YOUR COMPLETE GUIDE TO BUILDING A
MEMORY PALACE

YOUR COMPLETE GUIDE TO BUILDING A
MEMORY PALACE

GRAHAM BEST

Graham Best Academy of Memory and Learning

© Copyright 2018
Graham Best, GB
Memory Dynamics INC
Vancouver, Canada

All rights reserved. No part of this publication may be reproduced, distributed, or transmitted in any form or by any means, including photocopying, recording, or other electronic or mechanical methods, without the prior written permission of the publisher, except in the case of brief quotations embodied in critical reviews and certain other noncommercial uses permitted by copyright law.

ISBN: 9781090326300 (paperback)

Front cover image by: Loralea Butikofer
Book design by: Loralea Butikofer

Publisher: Independently Published

http://gbmemorydynamics.com/

Acknowledgments

I would to thank Loralea Butikofer for the cover design. She also set the book and did a lot of the editing. Without her this book would never have been completed.

I would also like to thank Neil Godin for his constant encouragement and wise advice.

I would also like to thank Sylvia for being such a wonderful and understanding companion.

Clipart images are by Getty Images.

Table Of Contents

Acknowledgments   i

Preface   vi

Introduction   viii

   The Tethered Elephant

   My Story

Chapter One

Leveraging Your Memory   1

   Picture-Association

   Picturing Anything

      1. Use words that have logical or obvious connections to the intangible word.

      2. Use sound-alike words.

Chapter Two

Introducing the House Method   5

   The house method employs two things we already know.

   We'll memorize the list of words by connecting them to each item of furniture in the order given.

   Let's do this with a room in your own home.

   Consider two secretaries.

Chapter Three

Memorizing a List of Names   12

   Let's learn the names of the Seven Dwarfs,

   Let's rehearse a little.

Chapter Four

Memorizing an Errands List   16

   We now come to our first "real life" application.

   Now review the first four connections.

Chapter Five

Building Your Memory Palace   21

   Use a Notebook

   Friends' Homes

   Vehicles

   Restaurants

   A Large Grocery Store

   A Shopping Mall

   A Park

   Your Own Body

   Review the steps

   How often can I re-use a room?

Chapter Six

Memorizing On-the-Fly (Mental Note Pad)   31

   Scenario #1 To Do List

   Scenario #2 Public Speaking

Scenario #3 Shopping List

Scenario #4 Topics of Conversation

Scenario #5 Useful Information

And even more…

A Fun Way to Hone Your Skills

Chapter Seven

Memorizing the Points of an Article   48

Article #1

    Step One: Find Locations to "Store the Information".

    Step Two: Invent a Picture for Each Statement.

    Step Three: Review the Pictures for each Statement.

    Step Four: Connect the Pictures to the Locations.

    Step Five: Review Until You Can Name Them Quickly.

Article #2

    Here are the points from the article:

    Let's find a picture for each point.

Chapter Eight

Extending Your Memory Palace   66

My Walking Route

    Find 14 Locations on your walking route.

My Driving Route

    Find 14 locations on your driving route.

Chapter Nine

An Impressive Memory Feat   85

The First Location

The Second Location

The Third Location

The Fourth Location

The Fifth Location

The Sixth Location

The Seventh Location

The Eighth Location

The Ninth Location

The Tenth Location

The Eleventh Location

The Twelfth Location

The Thirteenth Location

Conclusion   **93**

Preface

This book is meant to be a fun and entertaining read that opens your life to new possibilities. You have a great memory – there's no doubt about it. But more than likely, no one has ever shown you how to use it properly. I can show you how.

My personal mission statement is: "Teach with passion things that matter." I also believe that helping ordinary people develop an extraordinary memory matters very much. It is my delight to introduce you to a memory strategy that can enrich your life.

Students will get better marks by building a memory palace. People in the workplace will become much more efficient and will be able to easily upgrade their skills. Active seniors will see a remarkable improvement in their short-term memory. In fact, everyone can benefit tremendously, and I hope as you read this book you will find yourself having thoughts like, "I didn't know I could do that." Or, " I wish I'd known about this years ago." Or, "Wow! It's like a light suddenly turned on." Those are lofty claims, but I hear them all the time from people at my workshops, and I'd like to thank you for giving me the chance to prove them true for you.

As you work through this book, I encourage you to complete every exercise. Do not rush. When you master one of the exercises, move on to the next.

I also suggest you use a notebook to start writing down the things you are learning and how you learned them. I encourage you to search for opportunities to begin applying these principles immediately in your day-to-day experience. Have fun. If you turn these strategies into a game, you'll quickly discover the more you play, the stronger your memory becomes.

As a bonus, I have included videos designed to accompany this book. All of this material is visual and more accessible when you watch the videos and read the book at the same time. These two streams into the mind will reinforce each other, and the learning will be much easier.

So, let's begin...

Introduction

As I've already stated, this book could change your life. Yes, I know that is quite a claim, but it is true. To explain this statement, I'll begin with an old, and possibly familiar, story.

The Tethered Elephant

A young girl was watching the elephants behind the large tent at a circus. She was surprised a huge elephant was tethered to a small post by a flimsy chain. She approached the trainer and asked if the elephant could not simply break away whenever it wanted. The trainer said, "Yes, he could. He could break that chain as easily as you or I could snap a toothpick." The girl looked puzzled, and the trainer continued, "When the elephant is a small baby we tie the same chain around its leg. When it tries to pull away, the chain hurts its leg. After several attempts, the elephant surrenders to the chain and stops trying to pull away altogether. Now, when the elephant is older, it still believes it cannot pull away from the chain."

The question to ask yourself is, "What are some of the false beliefs I am tethered to?"

I have observed many people who become so used to their tethers they become unaware of them altogether until someone points them out. One false belief many people have is that they are not "smart" like other people, or they are average or less than average in their learning abilities. I meet so many people who believe they are stuck where they are. This is what limits them and holds them back. In most cases the root of the problem is they are convinced they have a poor memory.

This limiting belief affects much of their life. They do not move ahead in business. They don't pursue more education. They don't take courses that would help them. They become handicapped. Yes, handicapped! – by not remembering what they read. They are limited in their vocabulary and unable to express themselves powerfully. Like the elephant, they are resigned to their situation. They are unaware there is a way out, and they can break free. How? By training their memory. Let me share my story with you.

My Story

My background is math and physics (I taught High School physics for 39 years). When I was in university, I was convinced I had a bad memory. I took math and physics because they always gave us the formulae on tests. I didn't have to memorize a lot; I was able to figure things out. I avoided taking languages, biology and other memory-intensive courses.

Everything changed for me when I discovered memory systems. I'd had no idea there was a system to remember things. What happened to me after learning these systems was pretty amazing. I took Ancient Greek (intensive with all the verb endings), and I got 100% on the final exam. When I got that result, people said, "what a great memory you have!" but there is nothing special about me; I

Introduction

simply had a method – a way of actually approaching new material. I couldn't have done this without these systems.

What I learned opened up a whole new world of possibilities. I appeared on the old Alan Thicke TV show, where I memorized the names of everyone in the studio audience, and the last four digits of their phone numbers. After watching the segment, people thought I was some kind of special "memory guy." You have to understand: I was quite shocked I was able to do this. My passionate message to everyone is that **anyone can do this**! If I was able to do it, so can you! It's a matter of learning how.

Since that time, I have taken a variety of courses and have memorized extensive passages of text. Throughout my life, I've talked with so many people who have no idea there is a way to memorize. After just a lesson or two, they are surprised to learn they, in fact, do have a good memory, but they simply haven't been taught how to use it.

I've concluded the best way to look at memory systems is that they "leverage" your memory. Just as a lever can multiply or leverage a force (think of a car jack), memory training can multiply or leverage your memory. Memory tools and strategies can help you use your brain to increase your ability to memorize.

Since retirement, I now have the time to pursue my passion for teaching others these skills. In this book I introduce you step-by-step to one of these amazing memory strategies: **the Memory Palace**.

Chapter One
LEVERAGING YOUR MEMORY

Take a moment now to check out your FREE access to online videos: http://memory-training.thinkific.com/courses/your-complete-guide-to-building-a-memory-palace

Picture-Association

It's possible to multiply a force by using a lever. Every job requires the right tool, and the right tool for enhancing your memory is picture-association. This is the real secret to memory power, and it is the basis for most memory systems.

The best way to illustrate picture-association is to imagine an experiment where several word-pairs are slowly called out to you. (A word-pair consists of any two words such as "monkey-bike," "cornflakes-chimney," "ice cream cone-mouse," and so on). After thirty word-pairs have been called out, you are given the first word of every pair and then asked for the matching word. In our example, you would be given "monkey" and would have to respond with "bike." Next, you would be given "cornflakes", and have to respond with "chimney," and so forth. How well do you think you'd do if thirty word-pairs were used? The answer is, not well at all.

There is, however, a secret to achieving remarkable success with such an experiment. As each pair is called out, use your imagination to **make an absurd, exaggerated picture** connecting the two items. The funnier your association, the better your recall. For the word-pair "monkey-bike," you could see a monkey riding a bike.

The action of a monkey riding the bike places the two items together in such a way that whenever one is recalled, the other immediately comes to mind.

Totally unrelated items can often make bizarre and memorable pictures.

For the word-pair "clock-moustache," you might imagine a clock on the wall wearing a large pointed moustache. Maybe the moustache is replacing the hands of the clock. Use your imagination to see this connection. Take a moment and create this image in your mind. Try to see it as clearly as you can.

How much better do you think you would do in our experiment if you used picture association? I find people usually make guesses from 70% to 100%. The answer may surprise you. It is around 70%. Pause a moment to let that impact you. 700% better in recall! This tells me there is real power in using picture-association. But how can we tap into this? That's what this book is about.

Did you notice that every word I called out was a tangible word? That is, it makes a picture in the mind. The problem is most of what you have to memorize is not tangible. So, what good is this technique if it only works for tangible words? Let's take a look…

Picturing Anything

Broadly speaking, there are two kinds of words: tangible words and intangible words. Tangible words readily make pictures in the mind; you can see them and touch them. But, what do we do with non-picture, or intangible, words? What if the word pairs contained words such as "scientific", "abominable" or "contiguous?" Suddenly, it would become difficult to remember the word pair. Why? Because they are intangible and don't readily bring a picture to mind. In order to apply the concept of picture association, we must find a way to make these words into pictures. How do we do that? Answer: we find a picture word that will remind us of the non-picture word. There are two ways we can do this:

1. Use words that have logical or obvious connections to the intangible word.

Logical connections are made by using words so closely related to the word to be remembered they can be substituted for the word. For example, you can't see "time" in your mind, but you can see a clock. "Clock" becomes the substitute to remind us of time. "Clock" is a picture, "time" is not.

2. Use sound-alike words.

Sound-alike words are tangible words that sound like the intangible word. Here are two examples:

Suppose you met a man named Bill and you wanted to picture his name. You might see a dollar bill, a duck's bill, or a bill that you pay; these words sound like the name "Bill," and they are all pictures.

Years ago, I heard a radio announcer say that the new Premier of the USSR was Andropov. I thought, "What an unusual name. How can I picture it?" Here is what came to mind: I imagined a little ant walking across my roof, and it suddenly drops off the roof. "Ant drop off" sounds like "Andropov." Any word, concept or idea can be pictured.

The art of finding tangible substitutes for intangible words is an essential part of memory systems. It takes practice to perfect this idea, but it is a skill you can master. By the time you have completed this book, you will have seen many examples. I will lend you my imagination and you will soon be able to do this on your own.

In the next chapter I will introduce you to an astounding way to apply the concept of picture-association.

Chapter Two
INTRODUCING THE HOUSE METHOD

....

The house method is a strategy that will transform your ability to remember things. It is one of the oldest and perhaps the easiest of the methods to both learn and apply. In this chapter, I will describe this method and then have you try it. Make sure you actively do what is asked and be intentional about trying the exercise. I hope you will get a glimpse of your "memory potential" once you have finished this chapter.

The house method employs two things we already know.

First, it's easy to mentally recall the furniture in a room of your house. Second, we know that picture-association allows us to connect two picture words. When one of the words is brought to mind, it immediately brings the other word along with it: they are joined.

Therefore, instead of connecting two random words, we will connect a picture word to the furniture in a room so that a mental tour of the furniture in the room will then bring to mind each of the words we put on the furniture. To say this another way: we are placing things *on* the furniture as we go around a room, then we go back again and take them *off* the furniture. Let me show you how effective this is.

We'll use the room pictured below to remember the following list of words:

- gun
- knife
- monkey
- can of red paint
- beach ball
- toy car
- popcorn

We will memorize the words by connecting them to items, or locations, in this room. Look at the picture and note the following:

1. the empty wall on the left above the sofa
2. the sofa on the left
3. the decorative tree at the end of the sofa
4. the large window
5. the large mirror over the fireplace
6. the fireplace mantel
7. inside the fireplace

Introducing the House Method

Study the room and slowly repeat the selected furniture aloud, placing your finger on each piece as you name it:
The wall above sofa… sofa… small tree… large window… mirror… fireplace mantle… fireplace. (Note: when you select your furniture it is best to move in a general left to right direction as you proceed around the room. This helps to preserve the order of your list.)

When you can do this without a pause, you are ready to move on. (Note: this is much easier to do if you were to use a room in your own home. We'll do that in a moment, but for now, I'll lend you this room to illustrate how it works.)

Here again is our sample list: gun; knife; monkey; can of red paint; beach ball; toy car; popcorn.

We'll memorize the list of words by connecting them to each item of furniture in the order given.

Take as much time as you need to make the connections. Do not rush. Engage each description and give it your full attention. Looking back at the picture, make the following associations.

1. Connect the *gun* to the **wall**. Imagine shooting the gun and making bullet holes in the wall. Hear the sound. Take a moment to strengthen the association.
2. Connect the *knife* to the **sofa**. Take the knife and rip up the beautiful sofa. That is horrible! See the picture clearly.
3. Connect the *monkey* to the **tree**. See him climbing the tree. He stands atop the tree and begins to do flips.
4. Connect the *can of red paint* to the **window**. Throw the entire can of paint against the window. What a mess it makes!

5. Imagine throwing the *beach ball* against the **mirror**. See it bounce back at you. See how many times you can hit it and keep it going back-and-forth.
6. The *toy car* is on the **mantle**. See it drive across the entire mantel and fly off the end.
7. Imagine placing *popcorn* inside the **fireplace**. When the fire starts, the popcorn begins to pop. See it flying out. You have to duck out of the way. The popcorn fills the room.

Run through this a couple of times to lock in each association. Now, with picture of the room before you, name the list of words.

This was only seven words, but you could have memorized many more. There are more items or locations we could have used in this room, and we could have gone into another room and used locations there. In fact, you could quickly memorize 25 words or even 100 words using this approach. I know for most people, quickly memorizing that many words in a row, would seem impossible.

Let's do this with a room in your own home.

The rule of thumb is to move left to right around the room when you select your furniture. In the space provided below write down eight items of furniture from a room in your house, then spend a few moments to mentally recall the order of the furniture.

furniture 1 _____
furniture 2 _____
furniture 3 _____
furniture 4 _____
furniture 5 _____
furniture 6 _____
furniture 7 _____
furniture 8 _____

Here is a list of eight words:
- elephant
- hamburger
- moustache
- train
- bread
- glasses
- rocket
- grasshopper

Take whatever time is necessary to connect each word to the piece of furniture. Be creative in making your connections. Use humor if possible.

Now look over your furniture and name the eight-item list.

This simple exercise is the basis of memorizing important information in your daily life.

Consider two secretaries.

The first secretary has a large bin where she keeps papers. When her boss gives her important papers to file, she merely dumps them into the bin. Soon she has a large pile with no organization. When she is asked to retrieve a particular document she becomes frustrated digging through piles of chaos. So much time is wasted!

Secretary two has a filing cabinet. When the boss brings her material to file, she has a place for each document. When she is asked to retrieve a particular item, she calmly makes her way to the file cabinet and retrieves the paper in seconds.

Ask yourself this question, "When I put information in my brain, which person am I like? Secretary one or two?" Like most people, you are probably like secretary one when presented with information. You "dump" it into your mind with no thought of filing it for easy retrieval. I have some good news for you; using the house system is like making shelving space for your brain. You can place important information in your brain in a particular place and then retrieve it at will.

Anything important should be filed away in its proper place. When you need it, you know where to look for it. Memory is no different. Using this method, students at any level, High School or University, will know where to look for answers in their brain. In the workplace, you will be able to store valuable product information in your mind and retrieve it at will. In fact, anything you deem important can be stored and then recalled when needed because you know where to look for it.

In the next chapter, we will memorize an actual list – the **Seven Dwarfs** from the well-known Disney movie.

Chapter Three
MEMORIZING A LIST OF NAMES

In the last chapter, you were introduced to a remarkable system for memorizing a list of simple words. If you have never seen this before you should be surprised at what you are capable of. The problem, however, is everything we looked at was simple tangible words – picture words. In real life, most of what you are required to remember are things that are not tangible.

Recall in Chapter One we looked at a way of turning non-picture words into picture words. I suggested anything can be pictured. In this chapter, we'll apply what we've learned to memorize a list of names.

Let's learn the names of the Seven Dwarfs,

from the Disney movie: Snow White and The Seven Dwarfs.
- Doc
- Happy
- Grumpy
- Sneezy
- Bashful
- Dopey
- Sleepy

Look at the front of this home.

First, we'll identify the locations where we will connect our pictures.

Let's use:
1. the driveway
2. the front door
3. behind the front door
4. bush on the far right
5. inside the garage
6. on top of the roof

Note: location (3) will be used for two associations.

Place your finger on each location and practice reciting them in order until you can do it smoothly. You want to be able to say, "the driveway, the front door, behind the front door, bush on the far right, inside the garage, and on top of the roof."

Now we'll make the connections.
Standing in the **driveway** is a *doctor*. Imagine he has his white lab coat and a stethoscope around his neck. This will remind you of "Doc."

Now move to the **front door.** Imagine a large yellow *happy face* covering the door. The *happy face* will remind you of "Happy."

Behind the front door is a *grumpy old man*. He stands in contrast to the *happy face*. Not only is he grumpy, but he is also *sneezing* uncontrollably. This will remind you of the names, "Grumpy" and "Sneezy."

Now move to the **bush** at the far right in front of the house. We will make several connections to remember the next name, "*Bashful.*" Imagine a bashful man is hiding behind the bush. He bashes the bush and it falls. "*Bash fall*" or "*Bush fall*" will also act as reminders of "Bashful." Take a moment to lock in the connections. Review them up to this point.

Next, we go **inside the garage** where we find *dough*, baker's dough. The entire garage is filled with this dough. Someone is taking this dough and rolling it into little cylindrical shapes, then shaping them into the letter "P."

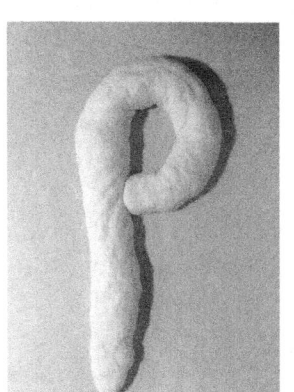

To picture the name "Dopey," we will use "dough P." Recall that "anything" can be pictured. You might be tempted to ask, "Why not see a 'dopey' looking person?" But, how do you know that he is "dopey?" You might see the image and think of "silly" or "funny." The "dough with the P" is out of the ordinary and clearly stands out!

Finally, imagine someone sleeping on top of the **roof**. This will prompt the name "Sleepy."

Let's rehearse a little.

Tour each of the locations and take whatever time you need to reinforce the picture. Do this several times and try to reach the point where you can look at the location and give the name.

It is important to realize what you've accomplished. With a little practice you can learn to picture any information. This picture can, in turn, be connected to furniture in a room. Tour the furniture and you have the information you want at your fingertips.

This opens up a new world of possibilities. Let's look at how to apply this to real-life situations.

Chapter Four
MEMORIZING AN ERRANDS LIST

....

We now come to our first "real life" application.

Let's **apply the Memory Palace** to recalling an errands list.

You might ask, "Why bother memorizing a list of errands? I can write it down." True, you can write it down, but it is not the best for your brain. You've heard the phrase, "use it or lose it." It is a fact the brain can make new connections and can grow new brain cells. This is exciting news for everyone! One of the activities that stimulate the growth of new brain cells is actively memorizing things. To put it bluntly, you need to practice memorizing. I can almost hear protests; "It's too hard!" or "I was never good at memorizing!" None of that matters now. Before this, you didn't have access to the right tools. Build a **Memory Palace**, and you will have the ability to memorize easily. You will be able to do what you couldn't do before.

Allow me to lend you another room for this exercise. Note the following seven locations as we move left to right:
1. Stairs (on left)
2. Large window overlooking river (this is a floating home)
3. Small bookcase

Memorizing an Errands List

4. Model of sailboat
5. Glass breakfast table
6. Counter
7. Stools under the counter

Study the following pictures in order to learn these 7 locations. Again, it is so much better to use a room you have been in. See what I have done and you will quickly get the idea and be able to do this with your own rooms.

Here is another view to help see some of the detail.

This is the situation: you are going out for a few hours, and there are errands you want to run. Here is your list:

- Pick up potting soil
- Deposit a check
- Pick up a book I ordered
- Pick up dry cleaning
- Mail a package
- Get more coffee beans from the coffee shop
- Get dog food

Let's remember these errands by placing them in the pre-determined locations. Take at least 15 – 30 seconds with each one and try to make a memorable connection. Be sure to look at the picture while you make the associations.

Dump *potting soil* down the **stairs**. Imagine the mess this makes. Take a moment and be intentional about seeing this action.

Imagine *checks* taped to the **window**. Each one is made out for a million dollars. Even better, imagine breaking the window and throwing checks outside into the river. Watch them as they are carried away down the river. Pick one of these connections and spend a few moments to reinforce it.

Look at the **bookcase** and see *books* flying off the shelves. You have to duck out of the way so they don't hit you. This will easily remind you to pick up the book you ordered.

See your *dry cleaning* as the sails of the **sailboat**. Hang the rest of your dry cleaning all over the boat.

Now review the first four connections.

What is on the stairs? What is on the window? What is happening with the bookcase? What is on the model sailboat? Let's continue.

Put the *package* on the top of the **glass table**. It is a little too heavy and the glass breaks.

Imagine *coffee beans* poured all over the **counter**. Or, imagine a gigantic *coffee* cup on the counter. Pick up the cup and pour the coffee all over the counter. Or, see a *coffee* maker on top of the countertop. Smell the wonderful aroma as the coffee is brewing.

See *dogs* sitting on the **stools** preparing to eat dog food. Maybe they have little bibs tied around their neck.

Now look at the room and recall the list. The simplest picture will remind me of the task. For example, when I see "potting soil," I am reminded to **pick up** some potting soil. I will know where to purchase it. I only need a nudge to remind me of the errand and my mind will fill in the details.

With the picture of the room in front of you, practice naming the errands a few times. It will now stick for as long as you need it.

Our errands list is information we only want to remember for the short term. So, if we don't go over it, we will soon forget the list. That is a good thing because there is no need to hang on to this particular list of errands. Also, we will be able to use these locations again and again for other short-term memory tasks.

Chapter Five
BUILDING YOUR MEMORY PALACE

You've now seen how to use a room to memorize. We now move on to actually building your **Memory Palace**. We can add room after room, and each of them will become receptacles where we can store information. They are like storage bins creating shelving space in the mind. You already have several rooms you can walk through mentally, but you need to know these rooms very well. You need to "preselect" and "standardize" the locations. You must know specifically what you are going to use in the room. This is a point that must be emphasized – **you need to know each room well**.

Note: You do not need to build your entire Memory Palace at one time. Start with two or three locations and "add on" over the next several weeks or months.

Use a Notebook

To accomplish this, get yourself a nice notebook and start making a list of the rooms you could use. Physically go into each room and spend time in the room. Make a list of the furniture or items you will use. Remember to move in a general left to right direction. You've already seen examples of what to use in previous chapters.

GO AND GET YOURSELF A NOTEBOOK AND START SELECTING ROOMS

Here are suggestions of where to find locations.

Friends' Homes

If you know someone well, you could ask to take a picture of a couple of rooms in their home. You don't want to be intrusive, but if they are friends, they should understand. I have several people I could go to and ask, "May I take a picture of your living room, dining room or kitchen?" Again, these should be rooms that you've already been in. You can add these to your ever-growing palace.

In each case you would sketch a "floor plan" and, if possible, take a picture. Write down what you are going to use in your notebook. Then review it occasionally.

Vehicles

You can also make associations to any vehicle (I'll illustrate this in a future example).

- car
- bus

- pick-up truck
- large U-Haul truck
- boat
- RV
- camper

If you use your car, you can make connections to the hood, the top of the car, driver's seat, steering wheel, passenger's seat, glove compartment, back seat, and trunk. This gives you eight set places to store information.

When you need to remember eight points for something, you can instantly access your "car" from your palace and store the information.

Restaurants

If there are restaurants you frequent, you are likely familiar with the general layout. Next time you visit the restaurant be extra attentive. When you are seated, take out a paper and sketch out possible locations that would be easy to recall. Take a picture if it is not too intrusive. It is excellent to add a restaurant to your palace.

You can use fast food restaurants.

Or you can use fancy restaurants.

A Large Grocery Store

There are many "super" grocery stores. If you regularly shop in one of these you have access to a larger "room" with many locations for your palace.

There is a particular store I shop at several times a week. Here is a list of the locations in order as I walk through this "super store":

1. Parking lot
2. Buggies outside where I enter
3. The enclosed entrance
4. The packed fresh fruit
5. The fresh soup
6. The salad deli
7. The takeout deli
8. The bakery
9. The fish deli
10. The fresh meats
11. The bread
12. More packed salads
13. Fruit stands
14. The aisle with the tissue
15. The dog food
16. The bottled water
17. Coffee
18. Milk
19. Cheese
20. Cereal
21. Cold Foods
22. Checkout

There are many other locations in the store I could use, but these are the ones I've chosen and know well. I will rehearse with these until I know them as well as I know my own living room. I want to reach the point where I can mentally walk through the store and name each location without missing a beat.

This means I have a "room" with 22 locations and I am ready to remember 22 things immediately. I should point out I do not necessarily work from left to right, but I remember the locations in the order I normally walk through the store.

You could also use a small corner store where you shop regularly. I encourage you to add a couple of grocery stores to your palace.

A Shopping Mall

I will provide you with two ways to use a shopping mall. I don't go to the mall often, so I have not added this to my **Memory Palace**. However, if you frequently stroll through a mall, you are likely to be familiar with the shops you pass in order. For example:

1. a bookstore
2. shoe store
3. children's clothing store
4. an umbrella store
5. a phone kiosk

And so forth.

If you can close your eyes at home, and easily recall the order of the stores, you can use each individual store as a "storage bin." Instead of using several locations within the store, you would put one thing you want to memorize in each store. This works very well.

Alternatively, if there are some stores you enter frequently, you could use each of these individually as a room with several locations. For example, if you often browse a particular bookstore, you find yourself becoming familiar with the layout of the store. As you walk through the store you might see:

1. magazines
2. check out
3. search kiosk
4. kids area
5. computer section
6. business section
7. wellness section
8. music section

Each of these would be a location within the bookstore where you associate information to be memorized. Once again, it all depends on how well you know the store.

A Park

Do you ever stroll through a beautiful park or engage in a nature walk? This too can become a location where you can store material. In fact, if you have any poems you would like to learn, this is an ideal place to "store them."

As you stroll through the park, you may select the locations you see in order. For example, you might pass a:

1. bench
2. flower bed
3. tree stump
4. small bridge
5. drinking fountain

And so forth.

Your Own Body

Many people use their own body to store something they quickly want to memorize. You could move from top to bottom and use:

1. Hair
2. Ears
3. Nose
4. Mouth
5. Shoulders
6. Hands
7. Stomach
8. Legs
9. Feet

This gives nine quick locations.

There are so many places that can become "containers" to store information:

- delis
- subway shops
- coffee shops
- donut shops
- hardware stores
- bicycles
- classrooms
- churches
- gas stations
- offices ...and many more.

Start looking for interesting places to add to your **Memory Palace**. Then spend the time needed to get to know the locations well. Add them to your notebook.

Review the steps

1. Use a notebook to write down the rooms you would like to use for your **Memory Palace**.
2. Write down the locations you will use within the room.
3. Sketch a floor plan.
4. **Take a picture if possible**. If you take a picture use your computer to print it out. Tape this picture in your notebook and review it occasionally.

The secret is to become familiar with the rooms you use.

How often can I re-use a room?
SHORT-TERM MEMORY

A room can be used over and over if the information you are placing in the room is only for the short term. Thankfully, the material will begin to fade if it is not reviewed or brought to mind again.

LONG-TERM MEMORY

Suppose there is material you want to retain for the long-term. For example, you might want to have a poem at the tip of the tongue. Find a room that is suitable and carefully connect your information to the furniture. To retain it for the long-term, you must review it often over the next several weeks. It is the reviewing that will secure it for long-term memory. You will find you need to review less and less over time and at some point, it will become a permanent possession.

Can you re-use this room? The answer is a tentative "yes." Do not re-use it until the material you wanted to retain permanently had time to "set" and become "fixed" in your brain. At that point, you can use a room again for temporary things. You want to avoid having two permanent sources of information in the same room unless one side of the room was used for the first information and the other side for the second information. In this case, they are separated, and there would be no overlap.

Here is another important suggestion. If you want certain content for the long-term, it is helpful to write it down in a journal. This will become a permanent record of what you want to memorize. You would write out where (room + locations within the room) and how (the pictures you created) material was stored in the room. By writing things out in a journal, you will not face the possibility of losing the information before it becomes permanent in the mind.

Chapter Six
MEMORIZING ON-THE-FLY (MENTAL NOTE PAD)

Let's look at how to remember things on-the-fly. Suppose you had a little note pad always available to you and you could quickly jot down anything you needed to remember. Wouldn't that be helpful? You would be able to recall anything you wanted to, whenever you wanted to, because of your ever-present note pad.

The problem is you can't always access a note pad and write whenever you want. It's not reasonable. For example, you may be driving. Your **Memory Palace** can become an ever-present Mental Note Pad. You can access it whenever you choose to.

Let me give you a series of scenarios and suggest how to apply the **Memory Palace** as a Mental Note Pad.

Scenario #1 To Do List

You are driving down the highway, and you remember several important things you've put off which need to be done today. You would like to write them down so you won't forget them, but you don't have a note pad at hand. Here's a sample list of what needs to be done:

- Make reservations at the Olive Garden (this must be done today)
- Call Mark (you have something important to tell him)
- Pick up a prescription (you will run out in a couple of days)
- Get stamps for your mother-in-law (you forgot to get them yesterday)

This is a very short list, but you know by the time you get home you may not be able to recall it. You may find yourself thinking, "There were things I needed to do. What were they?" You have no string to pull that will draw them out of your mind.

If, however, you have built a **Memory Palace**, you can easily access one of the many rooms in your palace and instantly use it as a storage bin. We'll connect this small list to a telephone booth. I know telephone booths are extinct now, but they are often my go-to for a short list of 4 or 5 items. I find it incredibly easy to use.

Let me lend you my imagination, and I'll show you what I did for the small list.

Please don't simply read this through, rather, commit to trying the exercise. Force your mind to work.

All you need is the simplest nudge to remind you of the task.

Memorizing On-the-Fly (Mental Note Pad)

Make the following associations:

- Throw *olives* on top of the booth. Take a moment to imagine this action.
- See *Mark* (if you know a Mark) talking on the phone; otherwise, use any other friend's name.
- *Stamps* are plastered all over the outside of the phone booth.
- *Pills* are scattered all over the floor of the telephone booth.

Go over these associations a few times. Be sure that you've captured them. "See" the action rather than simply "saying" it. Try to make it memorable.

Olives are all you need to nudge the action "call Olive Garden." The thought to call Olive Garden is in the mind already. The olives are a simple reminder.

When you see Mark in the phone booth, you will remember to give him a call.

Stamps stuck all over the phone booth will trigger you to "buy stamps." You will know whom they are for. If you think you might forget what is plastered all over the phone booth, extend the association further and imagine the phone booth is picked up and mailed.

Finally, you know how and where to renew your prescription. Pills are all you need to remind you to take action. Your mind will fill in the details.

Do you see how this "location" in your **Memory Palace** could help when you encounter a scenario like this?

Scenario #2 Public Speaking

Suppose you arrive at a function honoring George, who is about to retire. You know George well, and they ask you to say a few words about him. Unfortunately, they don't give you much notice; you have 10 minutes. What do you do?

Choose one of the locations in your **Memory Palace** and begin to think about what you want to say.

- You know George's family, and you want to talk about what a wonderful family man he is. To key this thought, imagine a *photo* of his family.
- The people do not know he is into fishing. You have some humorous stories you can tell about your experiences fishing with George. A simple fishing rod or a *fish* will act as a reminder.
- George's hobby is golfing. A *bag of golf clubs* could give rise to this thought.
- George wants to travel when he retires. An airplane could elicit this thought. Or, you could use travel brochures or a suitcase as a prompt. If you wanted, you could put *travel brochures in a suitcase* to act as a double-reminder.
- You want them to know George spent several years working in Japan. Imagine a pagoda or a familiar *Japanese car.*
- George is also active in a program feeding the homeless. See a *homeless man.*

All you need to memorize are these simple pictures: family photo; fish; golf clubs; suitcase filled with travel brochures; a Japanese car; a homeless man.

Since you already have details in your mind, these six simple pictures will prompt your short talk.

Once again, select a "storage bin" from your palace and place these items in it.

Suppose you've been on a friend's outboard motor boat. You decided it was excellent to use this boat as a storage bin for six simple things. You can quickly recall this boat and the locations you've chosen on the boat.

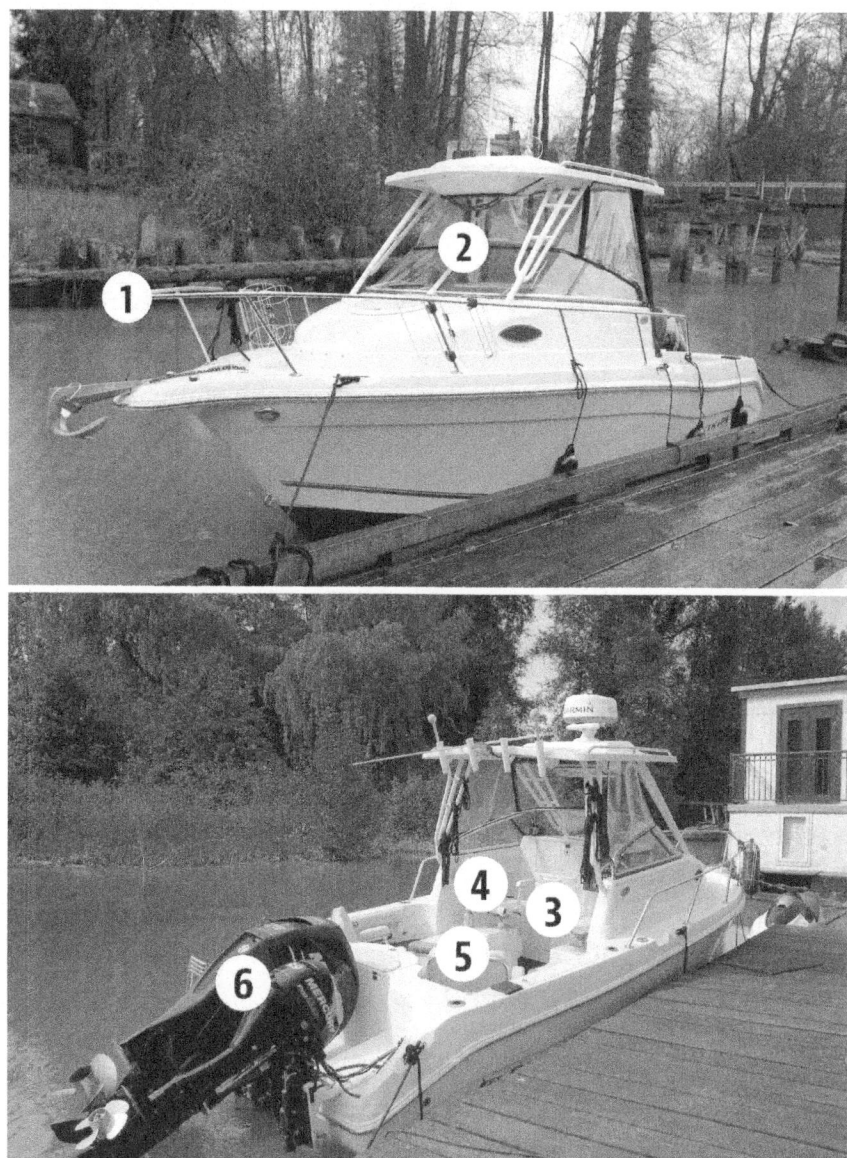

We'll use the following:

1. The front of the boat
2. Windshield
3. Driver's seat

4. Passenger seat
5. Back seats
6. The motor

With the pictures of the boat in front of you, try the following:

- Put the photo of George's family as a flag **at the front of the boat** (1). You can imagine a picture of any family for this to work.
- *Fish* jump out of the water and hit the **windshield** (2).
- A *bag of golf clubs* is in the **driver's seat** (3).
- A *suitcase filled with travel brochures* is in the **passenger's seat** (4). It splits open and travel brochures fly into the air.
- A *Japanese car* is in the **back seat** (5). When the boat accelerates it rolls overboard and into the water.
- A *homeless man* clings desperately to the **motor** (6) as he is pulled along.

Reinforce the associations and practice naming the main points of this impromptu talk by looking at the appropriate locations on the boat.

This works because you have a prepared "room" from your **Memory Palace**.

Scenario #3 Shopping List

You are driving home and receive a call (hands-free of course) to pick up some things at the store. At the same time you realize there are a couple of other things you would like to pick up as well. Here's a sample list:

- Lemons
- Chicken
- Apples
- Bread
- Milk
- Salad

Even with only six items, most people still think they need to write them down. We'll connect these to a car. Alternatively, you might think of the store you are going to and quickly select six locations in the store.

Let's put these in a your car, or a friend's car. Imagine:

1. The hood
2. Roof
3. Driver's seat
4. Passenger's seat
5. Back seat
6. Trunk

- A *lemon* is being squeezed on the **hood** of the car. You worry the acidity might damage the hood.
- *Chickens* are all over the **roof** of the car. You know when you drive they will scatter.
- *Apples* fill the **driver's seat**. You cannot enter the car. Maybe they are candied apples and they've made everything sticky. This is memorable!
- A *bread maker* sits on the **passenger seat**. It is making bread and the aroma fills the car. You love the smell of fresh bread. Bread may be too "ordinary" to remember, but the bread maker making

fresh bread, along with the wonderful aroma, is remembered much more readily.

- A *cow* is in the **back seat**. This will bring to mind milk. It might be too easy to forget milk, but the cow in the back seat is unforgettable. You even imagine the cow mooing, and you find it annoying while you drive.
- **The trunk** is filled to the brim with *bags of salad*.

That's it. It should take less than a minute to make the connections. Mentally run through them. Then randomly test yourself. What's in the back seat? The passenger's seat? The trunk? The driver's seat? The roof? The hood? That's enough to lock it in. Please try it!

Scenario #4 Topics of Conversation

Here's another scenario that I've experienced many times. Suppose you are going to meet a good friend for coffee. As you are walking or driving to the coffee shop, you begin to think of things you want to talk about with your friend. For example, you want to:

- Ask about their daughter Marsha.
- Tell them about a mutual friend you reconnected with on Facebook.
- Tell them about a stained glass course you took at night school.
- Ask how a meeting went with the doctor.
- Ask their opinion about you getting a dog.
- Invite them to a BBQ on Saturday.

There are six points, so you will need a storage place with six locations. Let's suppose you have a bus in your **Memory Palace**. Here are the locations we'll use on a bus:

1. Doors to enter
2. Bus driver
3. Front windshield
4. Pole
5. Seats
6. Back exit

Each of these would be a location where you store information. Once again, it all depends on how well you know the bus. This picture does not show you the inside of the bus, but I am assuming that you've been inside a bus and can relate to the locations within a bus. These are only my suggestions. You can use anything you choose both outside and inside the bus.

Here are some suggested associations you can make.
- Have *Marsha* **entering** the bus.
- The *mutual friend* sits in the bus **driver's seat**
- The large **windshield** at the front of the bus is made of *stained glass*. How in the world can the driver see clearly?

- The **pole** inside the bus has a *doctor* clinging to it. Be creative. Maybe he has his stethoscope and is trying to listen for a heartbeat. Ridiculous!
- *Dogs* sit in the **passenger's seats**.
- A man is at the **back exit door** with a *BBQ*.

Take whatever time is necessary to reinforce the connections. Look at the bus and see if you can recall your list of things you want to discuss.

Scenario #5 Useful Information

Sometimes you come across a series of quick tips, or useful information that you realize would be valuable to hang on to. I was in heavy stop-and-go traffic, slowly creeping along behind a bus. On the back of the bus was a list of diagnostic questions to determine if you may have diabetes.

Here are the questions. Do you:

- Have frequent urination?
- Have unexpected weight loss?
- Have increased thirst?
- Have foot pain and numbness?
- Have increased hunger?
- Have frequent infection?
- Experience blurred vision?

I looked at the list and thought, "I'd like to memorize these quickly before I pass the bus." My Memory Palace includes a gas station with seven easy locations I can readily use to store seven bits of information.

Here are the seven locations at the gas station:

1. The sign advertising the gas station

2. The gas pump itself

3. The nozzle

4. The waste bins by the pumps

5. A car getting gas

6. The convenience store

7. The air pump

I began working my way through the list of diagnostic questions, making up pictures and connecting them to the locations. I used the first picture that came to my mind. If I needed to, I could go back and possibly come up with a better picture, but all I wanted to do was capture the information as quickly as possible. Here is what I did:

Frequent urination
I saw the large sign advertising the gas station and immediately imagined it showing the icon for washrooms instead of gas. This was an easy picture. I then repeated to myself, "frequent urination."

Unexpected weight loss
I then went to the gas pumps and imagined doctor's scales in place of the gas pumps. Why would someone put doctor's scales there? It made no sense. This is an unusual and unexpected place for scales, but it worked. I repeated to myself: "unexpected weight loss."

Increased thirst
Next, I imagined the gas nozzle pumping out water instead of gas. An easy association! However, because this seemed so easy, there is a danger this would be the one I could potentially forget. I engaged the connection by imagining spraying water all over the station. I then drank some of the water from the nozzle. I repeated to myself, "increased thirst."

I reviewed the connections thus far. I tested myself, "What was on the sign? The pump? The nozzle?"

Foot pain and numbness
For this, I used my car, which was parked and ready for re-fuelling. I imagined my foot stuck under the tire as I experienced pain and numbness. I said to myself, "foot pain and numbness."

Increased hunger
I went to the waste bin next. It was easy to imagine hundreds of old "hungry man meals" overflowing these waste bins. As a "back-up," I also thought of a hungry man searching through the waste as he was looking for food. I repeated to myself, "increased hunger."

Frequent infection
"Frequent infection" was next. I've had an infected finger before, and I know what it looks like; I could use that if I wanted to. Or, I could choose to use any image of something seriously infected. Another possibility is to use a "sound-alike" word. I looked at the windows of the convenience store and noticed they were highly reflective -- they reflected everything, and it was difficult to see inside the store. "Reflection" sounds-like "infection," and I knew, as obscure as it is, that would work for me. Remember, all I need is a nudge.

Blurred vision
Finally, the air pump has a blurred eye-chart on it. Not only can I put air in my tires, but I can also test my eyes.

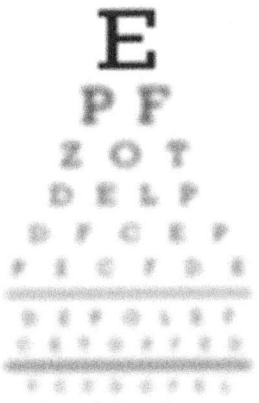

I then tried to name all seven diagnostic questions. I rehearsed them a few times over the next half hour as I was driving home. Later that evening I wrote them down in a notebook.

Study what I've done, then see if you can name the seven diagnostic questions for diabetes.

And even more...

Often when you are driving for a longer period of time, you do your best thinking. This is a time when you may get some excellent ideas. You can hang on to them by placing them in your **Memory Palace**. When you get home, you can record your thoughts in a journal. You may be formulating an argument about something while driving. This, too, can be placed into your **Memory Palace**. The possibilities are endless.

One particularly interesting application involves law enforcement. I regularly teach undercover police these skills so they can recall conversations while they are undercover. In their case, to store information in the mind without writing it down is a matter of life and death.

I encourage you to find situations to practice this skill of memorizing on-the-fly.

A Fun Way to Hone Your Skills

One way to practice is to listen to the hourly newscast. See how many of the "stories" you can recall. Don't bother with details at this time, instead, see if you can summarize the main stories, and then create pictures that you can quickly store in a room of your choosing. For example, here are some recent stories from a local news station and how I might picture them:

- A would-be robber was captured by armed neighbors and then left duct taped on the driveway for the police. To picture this, I'll see a man duct taped and lying on a driveway. This is a humorous picture and is easily recalled.
- A collision closed highway 3. To picture "3," I use a tricycle; it has three wheels. (In a future book in this series you will learn simple pictures for numbers. "Tricycle" is the set picture for "3.") To remember this news bite, I might see two tricycles colliding. The "tricycle" will remind me it is highway 3.
- There are no campfire bans so far this year. See a campfire.
- There is a search for a missing plane. Simply see a plane.

If you have difficulty picturing something, write it down and come back to it later. Carry it with you for a while and let it stew in your mind as you try to come up with possible pictures. By doing this, you will learn what works well for you in creating your pictures. Soon you will reach the point where you will be able to sit back, listen, and then recall all the news bites.

Make a game of it. This is a great way to practice.

Another way to practice is to memorize the order of songs from a music album. It doesn't matter whether it is an old LP, cassette, Apple Playlist, iTunes album or a CD. You want to look at the list of songs and see how long it takes to memorize the name of the songs and their order on the album.

The more you do this, the better you will become.

Be creative and practice these new skills. By exercising your memory this way, you are growing new brain cells. This is one of the best ways to keep your mind in excellent working order. Active seniors find that using these skills enables them to do now, what they couldn't do even when they were in their 30's. Pretty amazing!

Whatever age you are at, perfecting these skills will dramatically improve your quality of life. You will be able to take in information as never before, and as a result be more productive and efficient in so many areas. Your life will be greatly enriched.

Chapter Seven
MEMORIZING THE POINTS OF AN ARTICLE

Often I find an article that interests me and I want to remember the content. If I memorize this content, I can carry it around with me, in my mind, and easily recall the information to reflect on it whenever I want. This process will cause this new information to be assimilated into my life. If I find a particularly valuable article, I will write down the main points in a journal and then begin the process of systematically memorizing the main points. In this way, I am always learning and always growing!

It would never even dawn on most people that they could actually memorize the points of an article. But, with a **Memory Palace**, this is surprisingly easy. I'm going to give you a sample article that can become a model of how to do this. This is our most ambitious project with our **Memory Palace** so far. Ready? Here we go.

Article #1

Recently an article appeared that revealed nine risk factors accounting for 67% of all Alzheimer's cases. This is important information for all of us. Anyone at any age can act on this information now! Here is a brief summary from "Medical Daily" by Samantha Olson.

Researchers from the University of California, San Francisco, studied the similarities between Alzheimer's patients in order to flag risk factors so others can lower their chances of the disease. The findings, published in the Journal of Neurology, Neurosurgery & Psychiatry, reveal top risk factors responsible for two-thirds of the world's Alzheimer's cases. The research team analyzed more than 300 studies that focused on Alzheimer's disease-specific risk factors and narrowed it down to the nine they believed to be the most common:

1. Obesity
2. Carotid Artery Narrowing
3. Low Education
4. Depression
5. High Blood Pressure
6. Frailty
7. Smoking Habits
8. High Levels of Homocysteine (amino acids)
9. Type 2 Diabetes (in Asian populations only)

Here's the source for the original article:
Yu JT, Xu W, and Tan L, et al. Meta-analysis of modifiable risk factors for Alzheimer's disease. Journal of Neurology, Neurosurgery & Psychiatry. 2015.

What follows are the steps that will serve as a model for memorizing this article and any other similar material.

Step One: Find Locations to "Store the Information".

Once again, instead of a "room," we'll place the points to remember on a car. Look at the following picture:

Note: Normally we try to move left to right around a room. In this case, we follow a logical sequence of events. Every car has a hood and a roof – these will become our first two locations. You can use your own car, but I'll guide you through this by providing a picture. I enter the driver's side and use the seat and steering wheel. To my right is the passenger's seat. I will use this and the glove compartment in front of the passenger's seat. Next, I go to the back seat, and finally, the trunk.

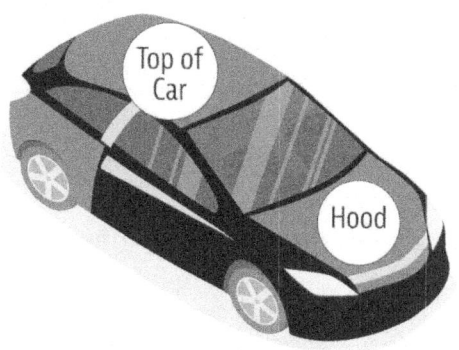

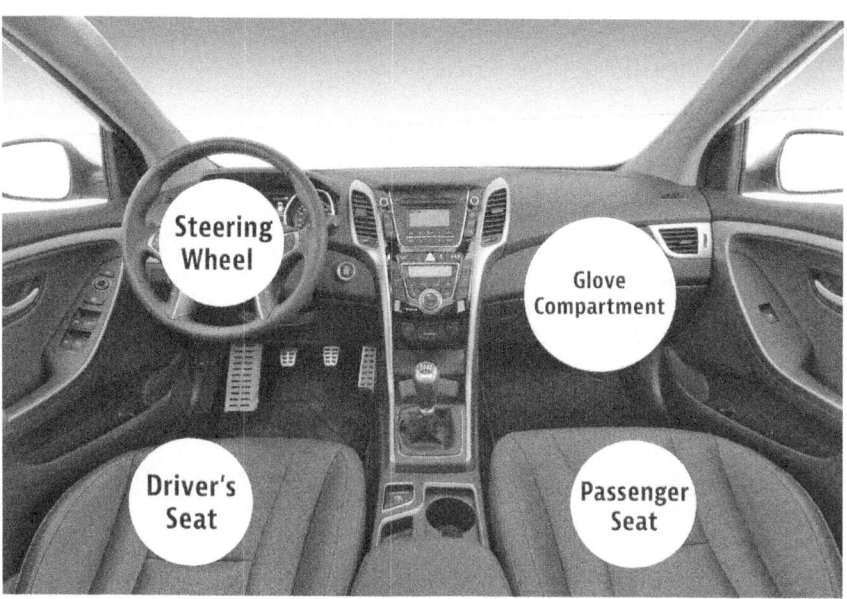

Let's review. We will use the hood, the top of the car, the driver's seat, the steering wheel, the passenger's seat, and the glove compartment. Take a moment to make a note of those six locations.

Now we'll use the back seat.

Finally, we will use the trunk.

Spend some time to rehearse those 8 locations; be able to name them in order.

> Hood – Top of the car – Driver's Seat – Steering Wheel – Passenger's Seat – Glove compartment – Back seat -- Trunk

Step Two: Invent a Picture for Each Statement.

These are the pictures I came up with.

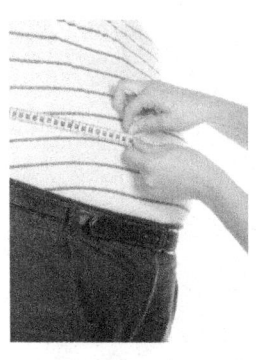

Obesity
See an obese man. You might even note that his large stomach looks like a letter "O." This is a further reminder that the word we want is "Obesity."

Carotid Artery Narrowing
"Carotid" sounds a bit like carrots. I will imagine carrots in a CAN. The letters in the word "CAN" will further remind us of "Carotid Artery Narrowing." (Note: the carotid artery is in the neck and carries blood to the head).

Low Educational Achievement
I see a "sad grad." She is sad because she did not graduate. As a further bridge to remember "Low Educational Achievement," imagine that her name is LEA. The letters in LEA will remind you of "Low Educational Achievement."

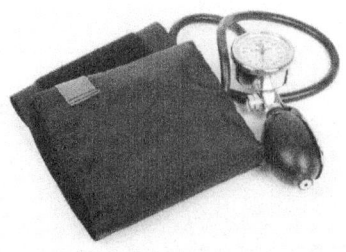

High Blood Pressure
To picture this see a blood pressure monitor.

Homocysteine levels

We will break this difficult word up into chunks that sound like the long word. I will use: "Home – Sis – Teen." When you say it together – "Home Sis Teen" – it sounds like "homocysteine" and this is easy to visualize.

Imagine two teens that are sisters. They stand in front of their home. Look at the picture and say: "home – sis – teen." (Note: Homocysteine is an amino acid in the blood. You can have your doctor test for this.)

Frailty

You can imagine a frail man, or you can see "frilly tea." This sounds like the word "frailty." See a teacup surrounded by frilly lace. Look at the picture.

Depression
It is easy to see a depressed person.

Smoking
See someone smoking.

Type 2 diabetes (Asian population)
See an Asian man injecting himself with insulin.

Step Three: Review the Pictures for each Statement.

Review by taking a sheet of paper and covering up the words in the right-hand column below. Read the statement in the left-hand column and see if you can recall the picture. Then slide the paper down to check and see if you got the picture correct.

The Statement	The Picture
Obesity	An obese man
Carotid Artery Narrowing	Carrots in a CAN
Low Educational Achievement	A sad grad named LEA
High Blood Pressure	Blood pressure cuff
Homocysteine level	Home sis teen
Frailty	Frilly tea
Depression	Depressed person
Smoking	Someone smoking
Type 2 Diabetes (Asian population)	Asian man with insulin kit

Now cover up the left column and see if the picture in the right column is enough for you to name the statement in the left column.

Step Four: Connect the Pictures to the Locations.

Obesity
Imagine the obese man sitting on the hood of the car. He creates a huge dent in the hood, and you ask him to please get off the hood. Look at the "O" his big stomach makes – this also helps to remind you of "Obesity." Spend a moment to clearly see this picture.

Carotid Artery Narrowing
Now, look at the roof of the car. See the CAN of carrots sitting on the roof. It is a huge CAN about 5 feet high. Notice the letters in C-A-N key off: "Carotid Artery Narrowing." Take whatever time you need to engage this picture. It helps to talk this through aloud.

- ❖ Review the first two pictures: What is on the hood? The roof?

Low Education Achievement
Now place LEA, the sad grad, in the driver's seat. Notice the letters in her name L-E-A key off "Low Educational Achievement." Spend some time with this association. Be able to look at the driver's seat and say: "There is LEA – a sad grad. That reminds me of Low Educational Achievement."

High Blood Pressure
Next, see the blood pressure monitor around the steering wheel. This is easy to imagine, but unless you actively "see" this and allow your mind to absorb the image, it will escape you.

❖ Review the first four pictures: What is on the hood? The roof? Who is in the passenger seat? What is on the steering wheel?

Homocysteine levels
Sitting in the passenger seat are the two teen girls. They want you to drive them home (home sis teen). Look at the seat and say: "Homocysteine levels." Take as much time as you need to strengthen this scene.

Frailty
In the glove compartment is the "frilly tea." The two teen girls take the tea out and give it to a frail man outside their window. Here we have two streams of connections into the mind. Talk this through aloud.

❖ Review the first six pictures: What is on the hood? The roof? Who is in the driver's seat? What is on the steering wheel? Who is in the passenger seat? What is in the glove compartment?

Depression & Smoking
In the back seat is a depressed person smoking. Imagine this scene!

Type 2 Diabetes (Asian population only)
Finally, there is an Asian man in the trunk with his needle for the insulin. Embrace the image.

Step Five: Review Until You Can Name Them Quickly.

That's it. Review the associations several times. Run through all the locations on the car and name the risk factors.

It is beneficial to place them on a flash card. Orient the card in the vertical position and write the statements down the card.

Put a cover card over the points and move it down to reveal each point.

Follow this model, and you will be able to memorize any points in any article.

- OBESITY
- CAROTID ARTERY NARROWING
- LOW EDUCATIONAL ACHIEVEMENT
- HIGH BLOOD PRESSURE
- HOMOCYSTEINE LEVEL
- FRAILTY
- DEPRESSION
- SMOKING
- TYPE 2 DIABETES (ASIAN POPULATION)

- OBESITY
- CAROTID ARTERY NARROWING
- LOW EDUCATIONAL

MOVE COVER CARD DOWN TO REVEAL ANSWERS

Article #2

Now I want you to do another article – but this time we'll use a room in your own home. Find a room that you know well and identify 10 items of furniture (or locations) in the room. Write them down below.

1. _____
2. _____
3. _____
4. _____
5. _____
6. _____
7. _____
8. _____
9. _____
10. _____

Spend some time reviewing these 10 locations. You need to know them extremely well — be able to recite them without missing a beat.

I read an article that suggested, *"The 10 Things to do Every Day."* This might be a useful checklist to mentally run through at the end of each day.

Here are the points from the article:

1. Get out in nature
2. Exercise
3. Spend time with family and friends

Memorizing the Points of an Article

4. Say thanks
5. Meditate
6. Get enough sleep
7. Challenge yourself
8. Laugh
9. Touch someone
10. Be optimistic

Let's find a picture for each point.

I'll lend you my imagination and suggest a picture. By observing what I have done, you will soon be able to invent your own pictures.

Get Out in Nature

Ask yourself, "What is the first thing that comes to mind when you hear the word 'nature'?" What comes to your mind may be the best thing to use as a picture. I will use a photo I took when I was with friends one summer. We were by a stream surrounded by trees. When I see that picture I will not think specifically of the trees or the stream; rather, the word "nature" will come to mind. Why? As I become familiar with this list I am memorizing, the word

"nature" will be foremost in my mind, rather than "trees" or "stream." So, take a moment and come up with a picture that would remind you of nature.

Exercise
I'll see someone exercising. As an additional nudge, I'll have them doing jumping jacks. Notice their body makes the shape of an "X" when they do jumping jacks. This will help key off "exercise."

Spend time with family and friends
Think of your family.

Say thanks
Here I'll find a "sound-alike word" – I used "tanks."

Meditate
Imagine a beautiful scene of someone meditating.

Get enough sleep
See a bed.

Challenge yourself
This statement is more difficult. What comes to mind when you hear the word "challenge?" The first thought that came to my mind was the old ad campaign: "Take the Pepsi challenge." Or, you might think of something specific that would become

your personal "challenge." Look at the picture of the man climbing the steep rock cliff – if that would bring to mind the word "challenge" you could use it.

Perhaps this word is best pictured by breaking it into a sound-alike phrase. I used "gel – launch." "Gel – launch" sounds like "challenge." This is so out of the ordinary that it might work quite well. Either way, pick one of these suggestions that works for you, or come up with one of your own. In the picture below you will see a tube of gel being launched into space.

Laugh
Imagine people laughing.

Touch someone
You may see your finger reaching out to touch a touch screen digital device.

Be optimistic
To visualize optimistic, I'll imagine an optometrist. "Optometrist" sounds enough like "optimistic" to prompt the word. Remember that you are becoming more and more familiar with the words in the list and optimistic is going to be ready on your tongue.

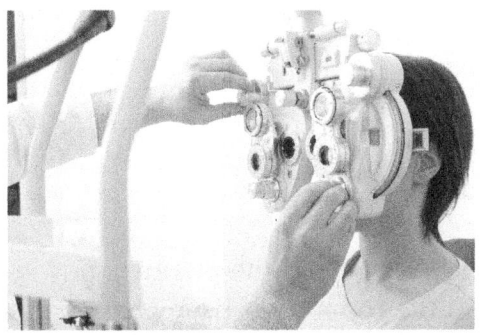

As before, let's make sure we know the pictures well. Cover up the right column with a cover sheet to see if you know the pictures for the statements in the left column. Then cover up the left column to see if the picture words give you the statements in the left column.

The Statement	The Picture
Get out in nature	A nature picture
Exercise	Someone doing jumping jacks
Spend time with family/friends	Family
Say thanks	Tanks
Meditate	Someone Meditating
Get enough sleep	A bed
Challenge yourself	Pepsi challenge; gel launch
Laugh	People laughing
Touch someone	Finger touching the touch screen
Be optimistic	Optometrist

I've suggested the pictures, now go back to the list of ten locations in the room you chose and try to make connections to the furniture. Go to your first piece of furniture. Connect your "nature scene" to that furniture. Take as much time as you need to secure the connection. Go to your second piece of furniture and connect the person doing "jumping jacks" to the furniture. Continue with the rest of the pictures placing each image on one of the locations in turn. Make the connection strong. Don't rush; take as much time as you need. Then try to recite the list. Rehearse it several times until you can recite it smoothly.

These two examples should be enough for you to do this on your own. The only problem you will have is coming up with pictures. I can assure you that you will get better and better with practice. As I've said before, make it a game. Have fun. Soon you will be able to memorize the points in any article with ease!

May I also point out that the skill you have just learned is an invaluable tool for taking courses. Night School courses, Online courses, or College courses provide the opportunity to learn new things, and this is one of the most important steps you can take to maintain a healthy brain at any age.
You have enough knowledge now to start trying some things on your own, and I encourage you to do this!

In the next chapter, I will show you an easy way to dramatically extend your **Memory Palace**.

Chapter Eight
EXTENDING YOUR MEMORY PALACE

....

Here is a variation on the Memory Palace that is very popular with many people. In fact, some find it the quickest way to input information and make associations. We will use a walking route or a driving route. The best way for me to illustrate this is to show you what I use.

At present, I live in a floating home community on the Fraser River. I can go for a walk from my home, up a ramp, down a path to the recycle bins and the garbage containers. I return by a different route. Here are photos of what I see. Each place is a location for me to store information. I am not asking you to memorize these locations, but only to see what I use for locations.

My Walking Route

This is a small equipment room. The table in front acts as a public area where people can share books and other things they are willing to part with.

This is where I start my walking route.

I use the bulletin board and the small table (locations 1 and 2)

I walk up a ramp (location 3)

Extending Your Memory Palace

At the top I find signage and a small equipment room (locations 4 and 5)

Across from the small room I see a bench and a cottage (locations 6 and 7)

Next are wheelbarrows to carry groceries up and down the ramp (location 8)

I follow the path to the left of the wheelbarrows (location 9)

This leads to recycling bins and garbage bins (locations 10 and 11)

I turn to walk back and I see a small house with a huge lawn (location 12)

I enter the parking lot where there is a place for wood storage (location 13)

Here are private storage units (location 14)

There are cars in the parking lot (location 15)

And finally, here is where we pick up our mail (location 16)

This gives me sixteen locations. I've walked this route hundreds of times and I can recite these locations as quickly as I can count to sixteen. When I need to remember a list, I will often use this route.

You can find many walking routes with several locations that can act as memory storage bins.

Find 14 Locations on your walking route.

Before you move on, try it yourself. See if you can come up with your own walking route with fourteen locations. You can select more locations if you wish.

1. _____
2. _____
3. _____
4. _____
5. _____
6. _____
7. _____
8. _____
9. _____
10. _____
11. _____
12. _____
14. _____

My Driving Route

Similar to the walking route is a driving route. There may be many routes you drive several times in a week. These too can become storage places for memory.

To illustrate, here is a route I followed every day for years as I drove to work. I am not asking you to memorize these locations, rather, I am only showing you what I use for a driving route. You will be able to come up with your own driving route.

I start at the driveway of my previous home (location 1)

I drive past the mail pick-up (location 2)

Here is the end of the street where I turn right (location 3)

I drive past a corner store (location 4)

I pass a church on my right (location 5)

I come to a main street with a traffic light (location 6)

There is another church on the left (location 7)

Then I pass a gas station on the left (location 8)

On the right is a bank (location 9).

On the left I pass an A&W and a MacDonald's (locations 10 and 11).

On the right is a Chinese Restaurant (location 12)

I come to a Subway (location 13).

Then another bank (location 14)

This gives fourteen locations. I know this driving tour extremely well and I've used this route as "storage bins" for memory several times.

Find 14 locations on your driving route.

1. _____
2. _____
3. _____
4. _____
5. _____
6. _____
7. _____
8. _____
9. _____
10. _____
11. _____
12. _____
14. _____

Take whatever time is necessary to settle on both your walking route and your driving route. Rehearse them, and in the next lesson we will do an impressive memory feat.

Chapter Nine
AN IMPRESSIVE MEMORY FEAT

Select either your walking route or your driving route and get ready to do an impressive exercise. We'll memorize all the countries of the European Union. Let me assure you that **you** can do this! Do you know your route well? Try to write it out by memory! When you can do this, you are ready to proceed.

You will only need 13 of the locations for this exercise.

Have your paper in front of you as we learn these countries.

The First Location

The first two countries to memorize are Austria and Belgium.

See an ostrich (Austria) wearing a bell (Belgium) at your first location. Make a firm connection. Have the ostrich ring the bell.

Notice we've placed two pictures on the first location – the ostrich and the bell. This is called "clustering," and is an excellent strategy to use when you have a longer list.

The Second Location

The next three countries are Bulgaria, Cypress, and Croatia.

We will now cluster three pictures. See a bull (Bulgaria), about to press weights. As he presses the weights he lets out a large sigh ("Sigh Press" will prompt the country "Cypress.") Now see a crow come and rest on one side of the weights (Croatia). Spend some time with this picture. Go slow. Don't simply say it; rather, try to "see" this scene. Talk through it aloud several times. Place this scene in your second location.

> Now name the first five countries.

The Third Location

The next two countries are the Czech Republic and Denmark.

Imagine a check (Czech Republic), written to "Dan and Mark" (Denmark). The check is huge. I think it must be at least six feet tall and ten feet long. It is also for a large amount.

Put this check in the third location.

➢ Name the countries to this point.

The Fourth Location

The next two countries are Estonia and Finland.

For Estonia you can use a "stone" or "stonework," and for Finland, you can use a "fin." Use a fin from a shark or a car. You can build a stone wall around the next location, fill it with water and let a shark swim around in it. That is one possible suggestion. Be creative and see what you can come up with.

➢ Name the countries to this point.

The Fifth Location

The next two countries are France and Germany.

In your next location see a model of the Eiffel Tower (France) with a Volkswagen (Germany) on top of it. Engage the picture.

➢ Name the countries to this point.

The Sixth Location

The next two countries are Greece and Hungary.

See a hungry man (Hungary) surrounded by several greasy foods (Greece). Have the greasy foods all over the location. See the man trying to eat them up. Maybe he offers you some food.

➢ Name the countries to this point.

The Seventh Location

The next two countries are Ireland and Italy.

For Ireland, I'll see a leprechaun, and for Italy, I'll see a bowl of spaghetti. See the leprechaun grab a noodle and begin to dance around the spaghetti bowl. Maybe you don't need a bowl at all. Simply place the spaghetti itself all over the location. See the leprechaun grabbing a noodle and dancing around the location.

➢ Name the countries to this point.

The Eighth Location

The next two countries are Latvia and Lithuania.

Let's find a picture for each of these countries. For "Latvia" I will use a "latte." As you become familiar with the name "Latvia," the latte will be enough to easily prompt the name of the country.

For "Lithuania" I will imagine either Shania Twain or Wayne Gretzky since both of these celebrities have lit an Olympic flame. You can use "Lit Twain" or "Lit Wayne" for Lithuania. It might even work to simply use the word, "lit." Do what you need to do to get the picture.

See either Shania Twain or Wayne Gretzky. Now put a latte in one hand and the flame in the other. This will give you both countries, Latvia and Lithuania.

You will need to talk through this picture until you know it well. Engage it! See the imagery and then describe aloud what it means. For example, if I use Wayne Gretzky I might say: "I see Wayne Gretzky standing on my table. He is holding an Olympic torch and a latte." "Lit Wayne" reminds me of "Lithuania," and the "latte" reminds of Latvia. Take as much time as you need to lock this in. Interact with the picture. Imagine asking Wayne Gretzky if you can have the latte. Tell him to be careful with the torch or he might set the location on fire.

> ➢ Name the countries to this point.

The Ninth Location

The next two countries are Luxembourg and Malta.

In your next location place a "deluxe burger" (Luxembourg) and a "malt" (Malta). Imagine sitting with a friend and sharing this meal.

➢ Name the countries to this point.

The Tenth Location

The next two countries are Poland and Holland.

See a telephone pole (Poland) with a windmill (Holland) on top of it. Or, you could imagine wooden shoes on top of the telephone pole.

➢ Name the countries to this point.

The Eleventh Location

The next two countries are Slovakia and Slovenia.

Imagine there is a mess in this location. You get a vacuum cleaner to suck up the mess, but it doesn't do it — it is a "slow vac" (Slovakia). You then take the slow vac and try to use it to turn a weather vane — but, it will not turn. It is a slow vane (Slovenia).

When I do this in my live seminars, there is some laughter because it is so off-the-wall. Interestingly, however, they all remember this one. Talk it through and spend some time with the picture.

> ➢ Name the countries to this point.

The Twelfth Location

The next two countries are Romania and Portugal.

Imagine a Roman soldier (Romania) holding a bottle of port (Portugal). Or, imagine the Roman soldier standing guard over a large Port.

> ➢ Name the countries to this point.

The Thirteenth Location

The final two countries are Spain and Sweden.

For Spain, I'll use a Spanish guitar. For Sweden, I'll use either the rock group ABBA, Swedish meatballs, or IKEA. Select the one you know best and create a connection to your final location. You might imagine the rock group ABBA doing an acoustic set with Spanish guitar. Or, you might see stuffing Swedish meatballs into the guitar hole. Or, you might imagine the guitar was manufactured by IKEA—and you have to assemble it.

There it is!

Now try to recite all the countries of the European Union. You will impress your friends!

Conclusion

You've now been introduced to the **Memory Palace**, and I hope you've come to appreciate how powerful and practical this strategy can be when you apply it to your daily routines. I encourage you to continue to experiment with this system and discover more and more applications.

For more information about my other books, videos and training workshops, you are welcome to drop by my website: http://gbmemorydynamics.com/.

It is important to realize some of the limitations of the **Memory Palace**. Someone asked me recently, "How would I use this to remember names and faces?" The answer is, "You would not use a

Memory Palace to memorize names and faces – this requires a different strategy." I describe this strategy in my concise, but informative book, *How To Remember "What's His Name,"* which is available, FREE, on my website: gbmemorydynamics.com. Included with *How To Remember "What's His Name,"* are online videos to support the content presented in each chapter. In this brief book you will learn the same skills experts use when they memorize a large audience. You may not need to memorize a large audience, but you'll be amazed at how easy it is apply these same skills to a small group! I had someone call and tell me they read the book in an evening, and then memorized a classroom of 30 students the next day.

The **Memory Palace** would also not be used to remember numbers. That requires yet another strategy. I will address this application in a future book.

Having said all that, I want to emphasize that your **Memory Palace** is useful for most of the applications you encounter in daily life.

Everyday applications include:
- shopping lists
- "to do" lists
- reading content (articles, circulars, instructions)
- conversations
- a mental notepad to remember "on-the-fly"
- inspirational material
- poems

As I have said previously, start memorizing things you would not normally memorize. Exercise your memory! Test your memory. Practice with your memory! An excellent attitude to have is this: make it a game! Allow me encourage you one more time: use it or lose it!

Students of every age and at every level can use the Memory Palace. Using the Memory Palace you will be able to recall:
- lists
- content within textbooks
- presentations

Conclusion

- pre-prepared essays that you think may be on an exam
- poems and other extended passages

I find that many students work hard, but simply do not know how to memorize. For many students, acquiring memory skills becomes the difference between average marks and exceptional marks. My full course on study and memory skills for college and high school students (or adult learners for that matter), is available at: http://memory-training.thinkific.com/bundles/study-memory-bundle

In business the Memory Palace can be used for:

- giving presentations without notes
- having product information at your fingertips
- recalling material for training upgrades
- reading content (circulars, articles, specifications, instructions)
- conversations
- motivational and inspirational material
- a mental notepad to remember "on-the-fly"

The Memory Palace is only one of several memory strategies that can help you. If you would like to receive a note when the next book in the series is available, or if you have any questions regarding my videos and courses, please email me at memorytraining1@gmail.com.

May your new skills help create a lifetime of beautiful new memories.

Thank you,

Graham Best

Do you find you have to ask for people's names, again and again?

Claim your FREE Ebook now!

Visit <u>gbmemorydynamics.com</u> for your free download!

FREE access to online videos accompany each chapter

Remember to claim your FREE access to online videos!
http://memory-training.thinkific.com/courses/your-complete-guide-to-building-a-memory-palace

Made in United States
Orlando, FL
26 February 2023